It is hard to think of a div
would lead to a more peac
the divide between Christi
accessible style that perfec

provides an exceptionally helpful guide for pursuing Christ-like relationships with Muslims. My prayer is that this booklet would receive the widest possible distribution so that those of us who call ourselves Christian would more closely resemble the Peace-making One we claim to follow.

—Rich Nathan, Sr. Pastor, Vineyard Columbus
Author of *Empowered Evangelicals* and *Both-And: Living the Christ-Centered Life in an Either-Or World*

Grace and Truth: Toward Christlike Relationships with Muslims is possibly the most helpful piece of literature I've read on how Christians can productively engage with Islam in general and their Muslim neighbors specifically. It's a clear and decisive call to Christians around the world to live out the way of Jesus in our ever-increasing tense global environment. Read it and pass it on.

—Carl Medearis, Author of *Muslims, Christians and Jesus*, and
Speaking of Jesus: the Art of Not-Evangelism

Grace and Truth: Toward Christlike Relationships with Muslims is utterly incredible. I would have given anything to have had this when I began to work with Muslims globally, but even more so here in the U.S. We will keep this well stocked at NorthWood Church. It's great for people, small groups, and anyone who wants to love Muslims like Jesus.

—Bob Roberts, Sr. Pastor, NorthWood Church
Author of *Bold as Love*

Every paragraph of *Grace and Truth: Toward Christlike Relationships with Muslims* winsomely invites the reader to reflect on what it means to emulate Jesus in his reconciling love in our relations with Muslims. A study guide with discussion questions provides a framework for vigorous exploration of the issues, challenges, and opportunities Christians experience with Muslim neighbors. The book is grounded in a commitment to Christ-centered evangelical witness and peacemaking; it provides the reader with insights into amazing possibilities for lively Christian hospitality with Muslims.

—David W. Shenk,
Global Consultant for Christian Muslim Relations (EMM),
Co-Author of *Islam and Christianity: A Muslim and a Christian Dialogue*

C

What a helpful, informative tool for Christians to use in understanding Islam and relating to Muslim neighbors. Using the Bible and the example of Jesus as the basis, this book demonstrates how we are to think, act, pray, and live peacefully with Muslims. With a study guide included, it provides a great format for groups in churches and other settings to use for discussions. I learned a great deal and am grateful for this guide.

—Dale Hanson Bourke
Author of *The Israeli-Palestinian Conflict*

GRACE AND TRUTH
Toward Christlike Relationships with Muslims

RICK LOVE

PEACE CATALYST INTERNATIONAL PUBLICATIONS

GRACE AND TRUTH
Toward Christlike Relationships with Muslims

Copyright © 2013 by Rick Love.
All Rights Reserved. Worldwide.

Published by:
Peace Catalyst International Publications

Arvada, Colorado 80002

http://www.peace-catalyst.net/

ISBN: 978-1-935959-50-2

Library of Congress Control Number: 2013950881

Scriptures taken from the Holy Bible, New International
Version®, NIV®. Copyright © 1973, 1978, 1984, 2011 by Biblica,
Inc.™ Used by permission of Zondervan. All rights reserved
worldwide. www.zondervan.com, unless marked otherwise.

Cover Design by Harmon Press.

Photos by: Mario Mattei., Mattei Visuals, LLC.
Used with Permission

Table of Contents

Foreword

Jesus was full of grace and truth: "The Word became flesh and made his dwelling among us. We have seen his glory, the glory of the one and only Son, who came from the Father, *full of grace and truth* "(John 1:14, emphasis added)

This one who is full of grace and truth calls us to follow him and imitate him. So the classic question: WWJD? ("What would Jesus do?") is not just some nice devotional comment. It carries ethical relevance for everyone claiming to be a follower of Jesus.

What would happen if Jesus' followers took this question seriously as it relates to Muslims?

We can take our cue from Scripture. The Bible demonstrates how Jesus would have responded to Muslims. The relationship between Christians and Muslims today parallels the racial and religious tensions between Jews and Samaritans in New Testament times. Both Jews and Samaritans were monotheists. Both Jews and Samaritans worshipped the God of Abraham. Yet the Samaritans were seen as heretics – syncretistic in faith, ethnically inferior, and excluded from the true worship of God.

The animosity and hostility between these two

communities is explicitly mentioned twice in the gospels:

> Therefore the Samaritan woman said to Him, "How is it that You, being a Jew, ask me for a drink since I am a Samaritan woman?" (*For Jews have no dealings with Samaritans*) (John 4:9 NASB, emphasis added).

> ...but the people [Samaritans] there did not welcome him [Jesus], because he was heading for Jerusalem. When the disciples James and John saw this, they asked, "Lord, do you want us to call fire down from heaven to destroy them?" But Jesus turned and rebuked them (Luke 9:53-55).

The similarities are stunning. James' and John's hostile response to the Samaritans did not reflect the Spirit of Jesus. And it sounds hauntingly similar to how some Christians respond to Muslims today.

Muslims are the new "Samaritans."

So how would our Master, Jesus Christ, have us respond to today's "Samaritans"? Jesus' interaction with the Samaritan woman in John 4 provides profound insights. A quick review of their interaction shows that Jesus demonstrated both grace and truth.

Jesus modelled grace by purposely putting himself among Samaritans. This is no little thing, since it was typical for Jews traveling from Galilee to Jerusalem to avoid Samaria like the plague. They would go far out of their way to evade contact with these impure heretics. So Jesus was being countercultural. He resisted the prejudices of his people.

In fact, Jesus actually engineered the encounter. He took the initiative to engage the Samaritan woman. Instead of the animosity or hostility typical of Jewish-Samaritan interaction, He began his discussion with her as a gracious bridge-builder. Jesus masterfully drew the Samaritan woman into spiritual dialogue by using a mundane earthly topic like water to point her to spiritual realities.

But Jesus was not just a bridge-builder, He was also a truth-teller, stating clearly that "salvation is from the Jews" (John 4:22). He didn't say she had to be a Jew to be saved though. Jesus told her that he was the coming Messiah. He was the Savior.

Jesus overcame religious, racial, gender, educational, and even moral barriers to connect with the Samaritan woman – to demonstrate God's grace and speak God's truth. That's Jesus one-on-one with the Muslims of his day.

In contrast to the fear mongering and the Islamophobia perpetrated by the media, this book describes a better way. It describes the way of Jesus. Read on and find out what it means to follow the one who is full of grace and truth.

Grace and Truth: A Behind-the-Scenes Look

The idea for *Grace and Truth: Toward Christlike Relationships with Muslims* was birthed during a global gathering of some fifty evangelical leaders concerned about the increasing alienation between the church (especially in the West) and Muslims. To counter this trend, we set out to create a statement on how followers of Jesus should relate to Muslims. Thus, this document focuses primarily on discipleship (how to live out our faith), rather than methodology (how to share our faith).

Though I am the lead author, *Grace and Truth* is a consensus document with substantial input from more than seventy leaders from around the world. My friend, L.D. Waterman, skillfully edited it – putting it through more than twenty revisions. We wrote both a detailed *Exposition* and an abridged *Affirmation*.

The *Exposition* is the heart of the *Grace and Truth* Project. But the shorter *Affirmation* functions as a manifesto. Leaders from across the globe supported this effort by signing the *Grace and Truth Affirmation*.[1] Here is a partial list of some of the original signatories:

- *Dr. Martin Accad*, Associate Professor of Islamic Studies, Fuller School of Intercultural Studies
- *Amos Aderonmu*, International Director Calvary Ministries (CAPRO) Lagos, Nigeria
- *Dr. Tokunboh Adeyemo*, (1944-2010), General Editor, *Africa Bible Commentary*, Nairobi, Kenya
- *Dr. Leith Anderson*, President, National Association of Evangelicals
- *Gary M. Burge*, Ph.D., Professor of New Testament, Wheaton College and Graduate School
- *Rev. Colin Chapman*, Author of *Cross and Cresent* and *Whose Promised Land?*
- *Dr. David P. Gushee*, Distinguished University Professor of Christian Ethics, Mercer
- *Dr. David Lundy*, International Director, Arab World Ministries
- *Peter Maiden*, International Coordinator, Operation Mobilization
- *Allan Matamoros*, International Director, Pueblos Musulmanes Internacional
- *Don McCurry*, Professor of Missions, New Geneva

4

Theological Seminary, Colorado Springs, CO

- *Carl Medearis*, Author of *Muslims, Christians and Jesus*
- *Rich Nathan*, Senior Pastor, Vineyard Church Columbus, OH
- *Phil Parshall*, Author of *The Cross and Crescent* and *Understanding Muslim Teachings and Traditions*
- *Dr. Imad Shehadah*, President and Professor of Theology Jordan Evangelical Theological Seminary
- *David W. Shenk*, Consultant, Eastern Mennonite Missions
- *Ronald J. Sider*, President Evangelicals for Social Action

The global impact of this document is noteworthy. The *Affirmation* has been written in six languages: English, Spanish, Portuguese, Arabic, French, and Indonesian.[2]

A Consensus Document

Grace and Truth is a consensus document. As such, it uses language and emphasizes themes that bridge the spectrum of evangelical thinking. For some, it may feel too conservative (with too much emphasis on "truth"). For others, it may feel too affirming (with too much emphasis on "grace"). The most important thing for us is to encourage evangelicals to address these issues biblically. I have told many people, "If you can't sign the document, let me encourage you to at least use it as a starting point for discussion within your organization!"

As an example of this, we have included the Peace Catalyst International version of the *Grace and Truth Affirmation*. We reworked the document to better fit our ethos as an organization. Thus, we have omitted one point and added two others points dealing with the role of government and terrorism. We also have included a study guide in the back to help guide you in your understanding of these important issues.

For the sake of grace and truth,

Dr. Rick Love
President, Peace Catalyst International
Consultant for Christian-Muslim Relations

Introduction

Jesus calls His followers to experience and live out the love of God, made accessible to all people through Christ. This includes showing God's love to all people, including those of ethnicities and worldviews different from our own. The gospel reveals that Jesus came to earth "full of grace and truth" (John 1:14). In that spirit, we as his followers seek to show grace and truth to all people as manifestations of God's love.

How can followers of Christ be people of peace[3] and faithfully bear witness to Christ in today's world? The threat of terrorism, negative stereotypes of Muslims, and ignorance sometimes causes the church to shrink back from fulfilling Jesus' command to love and to make disciples. Instead of loving Muslims as Jesus would and sharing his teaching, we too often perpetuate prejudices that only increase alienation and hostility.

To help us better understand Muslims, we will look at the beliefs of most Muslim people,[4] as well as those involved in terrorism. Then, we will seek to discern from Scripture how followers of Christ can interact with Muslims in a Christ-honoring fashion. This important task demands

Berean noble-mindedness on our part – eagerly learning and rigorously studying the Scripture (Acts 17:11). In the word of God, we can find discernment – that we might walk in wisdom and seize every opportunity for Christ, while not failing to recognize the evil of these days (Ephesians 5:15-17).

An Accurate and Discerning Look at the Muslim World

The media has bombarded us with sound bites and stereotypes. Sometimes we are told that Islam is a religion of peace. Yet the more disturbing and frequent picture painted is of militant Islam.[5] We need a view of Muslims that is as accurate and discerning as possible.[6]

The Venn diagram chart below describes the categories and population proportion of the various types of Muslims in the world today:[7]

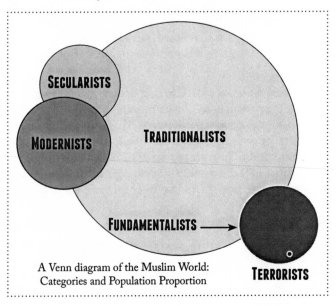

A Venn diagram of the Muslim World:
Categories and Population Proportion

8

Secularists reject Islam as a guiding force for their lives, whereas Modernists have a "West is best" approach to Islam. They want to change and adapt Islam to the modern world. Traditionalists view Islam as a source and treasure that must be wisely and flexibly applied to the modern world.[8] Fundamentalists are literalists who strive to obey the Qur'ān and the Hadith, while ignoring or rejecting many of the classical traditions of Islam. They seek to model their lives after Muhammad and his earliest disciples. Terrorists are militant Muslims who espouse violence to force all peoples to Shariah law.[9] They declare Muslims who think otherwise as apostates. Therefore, they believe less strict Muslims and all non-Muslims need to be coerced to submit to their truth, even if violence is needed to accomplish their mission.

We also want to address relevant questions raised by the Bible. The most significant question raised by the Bible is the one Jesus himself asked, "Who do you say that I am?" (Mark 8:27). Muslims have critical points of theological agreement and disagreement with Christians, and these are crucial to understanding their attitude toward Jesus Christ. Most Muslims would agree with us on the following important beliefs:

1. There is One Almighty God, who created the heavens and the earth.
2. God has given us commands and laws and will judge us at the last day. Human beings are sinful and need God's forgiveness and mercy.
3. Jesus is God's Messiah who was miraculously born of his virgin mother Mary. He is the Word of God. During his life on earth, Jesus healed the sick and raised the dead. Jesus is an infallible prophet (Acts 3:22-23).

4. The Torah, the Psalms (which Muslims call the *Zabūr*), and the New Testament, (which Muslims call the *Injil*, or Gospel), were (in their original manuscripts) the verbally inspired, inerrant word of God.[10]

Most Muslims would disagree with Christians on the following important beliefs:

1. The one God is revealed in Scripture to be triune.
2. Jesus Christ, the Word of God, is with God and *is* God. He is rightly called the Son of God (most Muslims understand this title in a literal, carnal sense).
3. Jesus died on the cross and rose from the dead. His death atones for our sin.
4. The biblical manuscripts are entirely trustworthy and the Bible that we read today is reliable. It has not been changed.

The areas of agreement are very significant and represent more similarity than the Apostle Paul found with the Athenians in Acts 17 when he made use of points of contact in his presentation of the good news about Jesus. The areas of disagreement are also very significant and include matters that the Bible holds to be necessary for salvation. Fortunately, many Muslims are eager to discuss these very matters with Christians, and both the Qur'ān and Islamic theological texts through the centuries allow for more openness and pluralism on these questions than is generally supposed. Sometimes face-to-face conversation with Muslims reveals that the problem (e.g., with the title "Son of God") is partly one of misunderstanding, not entirely one of substance.

A second question that the Bible raises ("Why do you

persecute me?" in Acts 9:4) can be applied to some Muslims' actions toward Jesus' followers (the church). Muslim attitudes toward Christians vary widely around the world, from Muslims who demonstrate warm friendship and respect toward Christians to others who cruelly persecute the church, and from those who respect the right of fellow Muslims to consider the claims of Christ to those who seek to kill "apostates."[11] Muslim attitudes toward Christians are neither monolithic nor unchanging. Muslim attitudes toward the church have often been changed for the better when Muslims have seen Christians living out the humility and love commanded in verses such as Ephesians 4:2, "Be completely humble and gentle; be patient, bearing with one another in love," and Ephesians 5:2a, "Live a life of love."[12]

Regarding questions asked by the news media (e.g., whether Islam is a religion of peace or of violence), we must first recognize that the Muslim world is extremely diverse. There are over 1.5 billion Muslims, comprising approximately 2,000 unique ethnic groups in some fifty-two Muslim majority nations, with large minorities in another forty countries. There are huge differences and varied expressions of Islam. Women, in some countries, are fully covered while in others they don't adopt a "Muslim" dress code at all; in some societies, women are omitted from the public sphere while they serve as heads of state in others. There are Islamic states where government and religion are intertwined, such as Saudi Arabia and Iran, and states with secular government, such as Turkey.

The Islamic World contains significant theological and ideological diversity as well. Islam has two major sects: Sunnī, comprising 85 percent of the Muslim world and Shī'ī comprising 15 percent, with several recognized schools of

Islamic jurisprudence.[13] Islamism[14] is on the rise, and at the same time, important voices in the Muslim world are articulating an interpretation of Islam that calls for peaceful relations with non-Muslims.[15]

Sūfism is a widespread mystical tendency, expressing itself through many diverse Sūfi orders and organizations existing within various forms of both Sunnī and Shī'ī Islam. Some estimate that as many as 50 percent of the world's Muslims may be Sūfis in the widest sense of the term.[16] The impact of Sufism on the various branches of Islam can be compared to the Charismatic movement's permeation of Christianity.

Even those Muslims, whom the media lump together under the label "fundamentalist" (a label often also used in misreporting about evangelical Christianity), are far from monolithic. For example, the *Usūlī* branch of Shī'ism dominant in Iran has a relatively high view of human reason in relation to divine revelation, as compared with the *Salafī* tendency in Sunnī Islam influential in Saudi Arabia.

One important issue to consider is that of *da'wa* (Islamic mission: the act of inviting people to embrace Islam). Most devout Muslims believe in *da'wa* and long to see the world follow the religion of Islam. A complicating factor is the assertion of some Muslims that "Islam is both religion (*dīn*) and state (*dawla*)." While these Muslims trace this understanding to the practice of the early Muslim community after they moved from Mecca to Medina, the political component of Islam has been understood and practiced in multiple ways in the various contexts and periods of Islamic history. Today the spectrum of Muslim perspectives and practice ranges from secularists, modernists, and traditionalists, to extremist Islamists who make their interpretation of *dīn* and *dawla* grounds for militant jihad. Most prominent Muslim leaders, however, have taken a strong and public stand against any form of terrorism.[17]

Most Muslims do not think of conquering the world for Islam. To the extent they consider Islamic advance, they think in terms of *da'wa* rather than violent means. Also, most Muslims are too busy with family and work to think about proselytizing non-Muslims. Just as there are differing levels of commitment to fulfilling the Great Commission among followers of Christ, so there are differing levels of commitment to *da'wa* and *dawla* among Muslims.

In light of the massive diversity mentioned above, how should we understand Muslims? How can we discern between the average Muslim and the terrorist? Colin Chapman encourages us to find a middle path between demonization of Islam and naïve political correctness:

> Many Christians feel that if they condemn the naivety of many secular people (and some Christians) who are willing to give in to Muslim demands/requests, the only alternative is to demonise Islam and take a hard line on every public issue related to Islam. A middle way between these two extremes would mean (a) being realistic about the real intentions of *some* Muslims, (b) recognizing the diversity among Muslims and relating to them as individuals and groups with openness and honesty, (c) taking a firm stand on issues of human rights, (d) working for the common good of the whole society, (e) demonstrating a fundamental respect for [Muslims] (without agreeing with all [the teachings of Islam]),[18] and (f) unapologetically commending the Christian faith through word and deed. [19]

C

Toward Christ-like Relationships with Muslims: An Exposition

As noted earlier, Jesus calls his followers to grace-oriented, truth-filled, and loving interaction with all people (including Muslims). We commend the following nine biblical guidelines:

1. Be Faithful to God's Truth – the Whole Truth
2. Be Jesus-Centered in our Interaction
3. Be Truthful and Gracious in our Words and Witness
4. Be Wise in our Words and Witness
5. Be Respectful and Bold in our Witness
6. Be Prudent in our "Google-ized" World
7. Be Persistent in our Call for Religious Freedom
8. Be Peaceable and Uncompromising in our Dialogue
9. Be Loving toward All

1. Be Faithful to God's Truth – the Whole Truth

We seek to relate to Muslims based on the core convictions of Christian faith, not by hiding or diminishing them. Relating to Muslims with respect, understanding, and love includes bearing faithful witness to essential truths of the gospel. Jesus is Lord. Forgiveness, salvation, and eternal life are free gifts of God's grace available to any person through repentance and faith in Jesus' death and resurrection. We seek to obey the whole will of God, with its implications for every part of our lives in this world (Matthew 22:37, 39; 28:20; Micah 6:8).[20]

2. Be Jesus-Centered in our Interaction

Our focus is Jesus because he is the essence of the gospel. God has revealed himself to us by taking human form. Thus, he can only be known fully in Christ, the eternal Word of God made flesh. We say with Paul: "For I resolved to know nothing while I was with you except Jesus Christ and him crucified" (1 Corinthians 2:2 NIV). We affirm a Jesus-centered approach to Muslims because it highlights the treasure of the gospel. It does not confuse the good news with Christendom, patriotism, or our civilization.[21] The famous evangelist to India, E. Stanley Jones, described this well:

> When I go to India I have to apologize for many things – for Western civilization, for it is only partly Christianised; for the Christian Church, for it too is only partly Christianised; for myself, for I am only a Christian-in-the-making; but when it comes to Jesus, there are no apologies on my lips, for there are none in my heart. He is our one perfect possession.[22]

Thus, we don't argue about Christianity versus Islam. We focus on who Jesus is and what he has done for us. As followers of Christ, our message and ultimate allegiance is to the good news about Jesus. Jesus is our model, and we seek to embody his life in all we say and do.

3. Be Truthful and Gracious in our Words and Witness

We seek to be accurate when we speak about Muslims and their faith. Overstatement, exaggeration, and words taken out of context are commonplace in the media and politics.

But this should not be the case among followers of Jesus, for he calls us to be careful about the words we speak (Matthew 12:36). God commands us not to bear false witness against our neighbor (Exodus 20:16) and to do unto others as we would have them do unto us (Matthew 7:12). Thus, we strive to speak truthfully about Muslims, *to respect Muslims' own interpretation of themselves,* and "not to compare the best of Christianity with the worst of Islam."[23]

Moreover, we seek to be clear and positive in our communication of the gospel to Muslims. We know that words can be literally true yet harmful. Thus, the Bible calls us to both truthful accuracy and fullness of grace. As those who have received grace, we are to convey grace (Ephesians 4:29 NASB). Not only the content of our message, but also our motive and manner are important. Gracious communication means our words should be kind and full of grace, even when we need to speak "hard" truths. As much as it depends on us, we seek to live at peace with all people, while acknowledging that speaking the truth will offend some – even when that truth is spoken graciously. As Paul says, "Let your conversation be always full of grace ...so that you may know how to answer everyone (Colossians 4:6 NIV).

To cite one salient example of problematic use of words, in recent years the term *islamofascism* has been frequently employed in public discussions of Islam and of various groups within the worldwide Muslim community.[24] In principle, it is not problematic to discuss the idea that some Muslims (or some Christians, for that matter) behave in ways reminiscent of fascism in certain respects. But using a term that binds the two together in this way may violate the biblical command for our speech to be "full of grace."

Many articles, books, and websites about Muslims and

terrorism present an alarmist and fear-inducing approach, focusing mainly on negative elements of Islam and the threat posed by radical Islam with its political aspirations. We recognize a valid role for identifying and monitoring the political and global aspirations of various Islamic groups, as accurate information along these lines should inform political policy decisions of the nations in which we live. We also acknowledge that respectful and gracious witness does not imply naiveté or silence about troublesome issues.[25] We are called to speak the truth in love. Yet we have two concerns about approaches that focus mainly on the "darker" side of Islam. First, they often tend to project onto all Muslims a radical agenda espoused by only a few, resulting in unnecessary fear and alienation.[26] Second, such approaches inspire many Christians to prioritize concerns of political power and self-protection above the commands of Scripture, such as love for neighbors (Matthew 22:39) and care for aliens (Deuteronomy 10:18, 19).

People like Robert Spencer[27] play an important role in exposing terrorism and thus potentially enhancing national security. His work helps inform governments, and we affirm the need for this. However, Christ calls us to seek first his kingdom – before and above national or personal security. Loving our neighbors, showing kindness to our enemies, and sharing our faith should take precedence over self-protection. Thus, truth and grace call us to a Christ-like perspective rather than a worldly one, in our attitudes as well as our words. As we interact with various sources of information about Islam, a helpful question to ask ourselves would be: "Is this drawing me more to defend my culture or to make known the good news of Christ's love?" The former is not necessarily wrong, unless in our hearts and minds it begins to eclipse the latter.

4. Be Wise in our Words and Witness

God's word calls us to share our faith wisely. "Conduct yourselves with wisdom toward outsiders, making the most of the opportunity" (Colossians 4:5). Paul's words and witness were also characterized by wisdom, "We proclaim Him, admonishing every man and teaching every man with all wisdom, so that we may present every man complete in Christ" (Colossians 1:28).

James described what this wisdom looks like in practice, "The wisdom that comes from heaven is first of all pure; then peace-loving, considerate, submissive, full of mercy and good fruit, impartial and sincere. Peacemakers who sow in peace raise a harvest of righteousness (James 3:17-18 NIV).

We do well to evaluate the articles and books we read and the commentators we listen to: to what extent do they reflect the peace-giving wisdom from above and to what extent do they take an approach of "earthly wisdom"?[28] We need to embrace that which is impartial and sincere, neither glossing over vital truths nor telling only one side of a story. God calls us to pursue the wisdom from above.

5. Be Respectful and Bold in our Witness

In the spirit of the Prince of Peace, respectful witness focuses on giving a positive presentation of the gospel. It does not attack the other or avoid presenting truth.[29] Respectful witness has nothing to do with being politically correct. It is a matter of being biblical. As the apostle Peter said, "In your hearts set apart Christ as Lord. Always be prepared to give an answer to everyone who asks you to give the reason for the hope that you have. But do this with gentleness and respect" (1 Peter 3:15 NIV).[30]

It is common to note the boldness of the early believers in their witness (Acts 4:31; 9:27-28; 13:46; 14:3; 19:8).

The Lord calls us to be both respectful and bold in our approach.[31] Yet many of us tend to fall short on one side or the other (or both!). One biblical example can help us see the model more concretely. In his ministry at Athens, Paul the apostle demonstrated that both are possible. The idolatry of the Athenians incensed Paul's monotheistic heart –"His spirit was being provoked within him as he was observing the city full of idols" (Acts 17:16). Nevertheless, he showed a respectful, gracious, and bridge-building approach to the Athenians. He affirmed their religiosity (17:22), used an altar as a point of contact (17:23), and quoted their own poets to help clarify the meaning of the good news (17:28). Then he also boldly called the Athenians to repent because of coming judgment (17:30-31). This fits with the engagement model commended by leaders of fifty-five Christian organizations from nineteen countries, in the statement, "Why Do We Share the Good News About Jesus with All Peoples, Including Muslims?"[32]

6. Be Prudent in our Google-ized World

In the past, when leaders in a religious community spoke, only their own community heard it. But today our words ricochet around the world. Perhaps the most powerful example of an interconnected world is the Internet search engine, Google. Type in a few words about anything and you can get a string of articles and information in seconds. In this "Google-ized" world – when we try to explain who we are, what we believe, what we do, and why we do it – our words may reach beyond our primary audience and enter the global marketplace of ideas.

In many cases, negative words merely offend, stir up hatred, or cause division. But in other cases they lead to death. For example, a well-known fundamentalist Christian preacher called the Prophet Muhammad a terrorist. One result: in Solapar, India, what started as a protest against this pastor turned into a deadly riot that killed eight and injured ninety.[33]

After saying something controversial, an outspoken leader may try to clarify his statement. But the damage is already done. Words are powerful. Prudence is required. "A man of knowledge uses words with restraint" (Proverbs 17:27).

7. Be Persistent in our Call for Religious Freedom

We affirm the right of religious freedom for every person and community. We defend the right of Muslims to express their faith respectfully among Christians and of Christians to express their faith respectfully among Muslims. Moreover, we affirm the right of Muslims and Christians alike to change religious beliefs, practices, and/or affiliations according to their conscience. Thus, we stand against all forms of religious persecution toward Muslims, Christians, or anyone else. God desires all people to make faith choices based on personal conscience and conviction rather than any form of coercion or violence (2 Corinthians 4:2).

We concur with John Piper's incisive rationale for this perspective:

Christians are tolerant of other faiths not because there is no absolute truth or that all faiths are equally valuable, but because the one who is Absolute Truth, Jesus Christ, forbids the spread of his truth by the sword. Christian tolerance is the commitment that keeps lovers of competing faiths from killing each other. Christian tolerance is the principle that puts freedom above forced conversion, because it's rooted in the conviction that forced conversion is no conversion at all. Freedom to preach, to teach, to publish, to assemble for worship—these convictions flow from the essence of the Christian faith. Therefore we protect it for all.[34]

8. Be Peaceable and Uncompromising in our Dialogue

Dialogue between Muslims and Christians provides us with opportunities to understand Muslims, build relationships, engage in peacemaking, and share our faith.[35] We seek to share the gospel respectfully and boldly, without compromise. We believe an important part of dialogue is explaining why the "good news" is good news![36]

Through dialogue, we work toward mutual respect, graciously bearing witness to our faith and working toward religious freedom. Ultimately, we long to see as many as possible reconciled with God, through the person of Christ.

9. Be Loving toward All

As Jesus made clear in his answer to the question, "Who is my neighbor?" (Luke 10:29), neighbors include people of different ethnicities and religious views – not just those who live near us, but anyone with whom the Lord might bring us into contact. The command of God to his people stands for all time: "Love your neighbor as yourself" (Leviticus 19:18; Luke 10:27b).

The abominable terrorist acts around the world (in both Western and Muslim countries including the United States, the United Kingdom, Spain, Jordan, Egypt, Turkey, Morocco, Indonesia, and India) along with the continuing threat of terrorist attacks, create profound security challenges. These terrorist acts also fuel negative attitudes toward Muslims. Yet most of the world's Muslims are not our enemies.

How can a follower of Christ take seriously Jesus' commands to love our neighbor and love our enemy and yet address the real threat of terrorism? Jesus' teaching about love of enemy (Luke 6:35) is among the most radical and most ignored commands in the Bible. Many Christians think this command reflects an unrealistic and idealistic standard. Yet we need to not engage in the "hermeneutics of evasion"[37] – figuring out ways to interpret Jesus' command so it doesn't apply to our lives.[38]

We find a striking parallel between being a peacemaker (Matthew 5:9) and loving one's enemies. Both peacemakers and those who love their enemies are described as "sons [or daughters] of God" (Matthew 5:9, 44; Luke 6:35). They are called children of God because they are acting like their Father: the God of Peace (Philippians 4:9; 1 Thessalonians 5:23) who sent the Prince of Peace (Isaiah 9:6) to bring about a world of peace (Luke 2:14). Peacemakers and those who love their enemies demonstrate their authenticity as children of God by their words and acts of peace.

Both Jesus and Paul gave numerous practical commands concerning love for enemies:

- Do good to those who hate you,
- Bless those who curse you,
- Pray for those who mistreat you,
- Lend to others without expecting them to pay it back,
- Feed those who are hungry,
- Give a drink to the thirsty, and
- Overcome evil with good (see Matt 5:39-48; Luke 6:27-36 and Romans 12:17-21).

These commands demonstrate that "loving our enemy" should not be interpreted in sentimental terms. In this context, love refers to acts of kindness. These acts of kindness describe what some call "transforming initiatives,"[39] that is, they help bring deliverance from the vicious cycle of hostility and violence. As Richard Hays notes:

By doing more than the oppressor requires, the disciples bear witness to another reality (the kingdom of God), a reality in which peacefulness, service, and generosity are valued above self-defense and personal rights. Thus, the prophetic nonresistance of the community may not only confound the enemy but also pose an opportunity for the enemy to be converted to the truth of God's kingdom.[40]

The command to "love your enemy" comes from the one who modeled love for enemies. Jesus loved us and laid down his life for us "while we were enemies" (Romans 5:10; cf. Colossians 1:21). After His enemies nailed him to the cross, he prayed, "Father forgive them; for they do not know what they are doing" (Luke 23:34). Responding to enemies with self-giving, sacrificial love demonstrates the gospel.[41]

Conclusion

We have been entrusted with the ministry of reconciliation and are commanded to make known the gospel "in season and out of season" (2 Corinthians 5:18,19; 2 Timothy 4:2). The commission to "make disciples of all nations" has not been rescinded. Neither have the commands to demonstrate sacrificial love and to work toward peace. We may differ on our views of Islam and how to oppose or minimize acts of terror, but we can agree that there is no separate gospel for wartime and peacetime. The message of God's love in Christ is for all times, places, and peoples.

We believe the nine biblical guidelines outlined in this exposition can help us as followers of Christ to remain faithful to him and become more fruitful in our relationships with Muslims. We desire to live out and share the truth of Christ in ways that are filled with grace. In these difficult times, we face great challenges, but we also enjoy extraordinary opportunities. Let us use these opportunities to show forth the grace and truth of our Lord Jesus Christ.

C

Toward Christ-like Relationships with Muslims: An Affirmation

(The Peace Catalyst International Version)

Jesus was full of grace and truth (John 1:14). As his followers, we aspire to walk in the fullness of grace and truth in our relationships with Muslims. We seek to be agents of peace in a polarized world.

Together Christians and Muslims make up over half of the human race. Thus, peaceful relations between these faith communities stand as one of the central challenges of this century. But the pathway to peace faces troublesome obstacles.

The relationship between Christians and Muslims is supercharged by "war on terror" and exacerbated by the fact that western countries are perceived as "Christian" by many Muslims. The threat of terrorism, negative stereotypes of Muslims, and ignorance have caused the church to shrink back from obeying the fundamental biblical commands to love and bear witness.

Moreover, just as there is significant theological, cultural, and ideological diversity among Christians, so, too, is there among Muslims. The spectrum of Muslim perspectives and practices range from secularists, modernists, traditionalists, and fundamentalists, to a miniscule minority of violent extremists.

It has been our privilege to enjoy warm hospitality and deep interaction with Muslims around the world. They are neighbors, friends, and colleagues who have challenged, clarified, and encouraged our thinking about peacemaking.

In honor of Jesus Christ, the Prince of Peace, Peace Catalyst International affirms ten biblical guidelines that will enable Jesus' followers to serve as his representatives in relationship with Muslims of every persuasion. The following guidelines grow out of the Grace and Truth Project, reflecting Peace Catalyst's revised, personalized version of these affirmations.

1. Be Jesus-Centered in our Interaction
2. Be Truthful and Gracious in our Words and Witness
3. Be Wise in our Words and Witness
4. Be Respectful and Bold in our Witness
5. Be Prudent in our Glocalized World
6. Be Persistent in our Call for Religious Freedom
7. Be Peaceable and Uncompromising in our Dialogue
8. Be Loving toward All
9. Differentiate between the Role of Church and State
10. Support and Challenge the State

1. Be Jesus-Centered in our Interaction

Our focus is Jesus because he is the heart of the gospel. We say as Paul did, "For I resolved to know nothing while I was with you except Jesus Christ and him crucified" (1 Corinthians 2:2 NIV). We affirm a Jesus-centered approach to Muslims because it highlights the treasure of the gospel. It does not confuse the good news with Christendom, patriotism, or our civilization.

Therefore, we seek to keep Jesus at the center of our lives, conversations, and relationships with Muslims.

2. Be Truthful and Gracious in our Words and Witness

We seek to be accurate when we speak about Muslims and their faith. Overstatement, exaggeration, and words taken out of context should not be found among followers of Jesus, for he calls us to be careful about the words we speak (Matthew 12:36). God commands us not to bear false witness against our neighbor (Exodus 20:16) and to do unto others as we would have them do unto us (Matthew 7:12). Thus, we strive to speak truthfully about Muslims, *to respect Muslims' own interpretation of themselves,* and not to compare the best interpretation and practice of our faith with the worst interpretation and practice of theirs.

The content of our message is important, and so is how we convey it. As those who have received grace, we are to convey grace (Ephesians 4:29 NASB). Paul says, "Let your conversation be always full of grace …so that you may know how to answer everyone (Colossians 4:6 NIV). The Bible calls us to truthful accuracy and fullness of grace.

Therefore, we seek to be accurate and positive in our witness. We also seek to be gracious in our communication, using kind words, even when we need to speak "hard" truths.

3. Be Wise in our Words and Witness

God's Word calls us to walk in wisdom and to share our faith wisely. "Conduct yourselves with wisdom toward outsiders, making the most of the opportunity" (Colossians 4:5). What does wisdom look like in practice?

According to James, "the wisdom that comes from heaven

is first of all pure; then peace-loving, considerate, submissive, full of mercy and good fruit, impartial, and sincere. Peacemakers who sow in peace raise a harvest of righteousness" (James 3:17-18 NIV). Peace is the ruling idea in this passage. According to James, heavenly wisdom creates a peacemaking community.

Therefore, we seek to walk in God's peace-producing wisdom.

4. Be Respectful and Bold in our Witness

In the spirit of the Prince of Peace, respectful witness focuses on giving a positive presentation of the gospel. It does not attack the other or avoid presenting truth. As the apostle Peter said, "In your hearts set apart Christ as Lord. Always be prepared to give an answer to everyone who asks you to give the reason for the hope that you have. But do this with gentleness and respect" (1 Peter 3:15 NIV). Numerous biblical examples (i.e., Acts 4:31; 9:27-28; 13:46; 14:3; 17:30-31; 19:8) invite us to emulate the boldness of early followers of Jesus in sharing the good news.

Therefore, in obedience to the Scripture, we seek to be both respectful and bold in our witness.

5. Be Prudent in our "Glocalized"[42] World

In the past, what we spoke to our community stayed in our community. But due to the Internet, today our words ricochet around the world, for good or for bad. When we try to explain who we are, what we believe, what we do, and why we do it, our words may reach beyond our primary audience and enter the global marketplace of ideas. After saying something hurtful (whether intentional or not), we may try to clarify our statement. But the damage is already done. Conversely, when we say something positive, the kindness of our words may extend way beyond the circle of our community. Words are powerful.

Therefore, we seek to be prudent in our communication. A truly wise person uses few words (Proverbs 17:27 NLT).

6. Be Persistent in our Call for Religious Freedom

We affirm the right of religious freedom for every person and community. We defend the right of Muslims to express their faith respectfully among Christians and of Christians to express their faith respectfully among Muslims. Moreover, we affirm the right of Muslims and Christians alike to change religious beliefs, practices, and/or affiliations according to their conscience (2 Corinthians 4:2). Thus, we stand against all forms of religious persecution toward Muslims, Christians, or anyone else.

We concur with Pastor John Piper's incisive rationale for this perspective:

> Christians are tolerant of other faiths not because there is no absolute truth or that all faiths are equally valuable, but because the one who is Absolute Truth, Jesus Christ, forbids the spread of his truth by the sword. Christian tolerance is the commitment that keeps lovers of competing faiths from killing each other. Christian tolerance is the principle that puts freedom above forced conversion, because it's rooted in the conviction that forced conversion is no conversion at all. Freedom to preach, to teach, to publish, to assemble for worship—these convictions flow from the essence of the Christian faith. Therefore we protect it for all.[43]

Therefore, we strive to protect religious freedom for all.

7. Be Peaceable and Uncompromising in our Dialogue

Dialogue between Muslims and Christians provides us

with opportunities to understand Muslims, build relationships, engage in peacemaking, and share an accurate explanation of our faith. Through dialogue, we seek to reframe the Muslim-Christian relationship so it is no longer perceived as a "clash of civilizations."

But this does not mean we dissolve our distinctive, historic beliefs into an imaginary "One World Religion." Rather, it means each community seeks to be authentically faithful to their historic beliefs and finds *within* those beliefs the resources to reach out to one another in love.

Therefore, we strive to work toward mutual respect, graciously bearing witness to our faith, and working toward religious freedom.

8. Be Loving toward All

The world's Muslims are our neighbors, as Jesus used the term (Luke 10:29-37). The command of God to his people stands for all time, "Love your neighbor as yourself" (Leviticus 19:18; Luke 10:27b). How can a follower of Christ take seriously Jesus' command to love our neighbor and, at the same time, address the real threat of terrorism by those who position themselves as our enemies? Jesus' teaching about love of enemy (Luke 6:35) is among the most radical and most ignored commands in the Bible. We do not want to engage in the "hermeneutics of evasion"– figuring out ways to interpret Jesus' command so it doesn't apply to our lives.

Both peacemakers and those who love their enemies are described as "sons [or daughters] of God" (Matthew 5:9, 44; Luke 6:35). They are called children of God because they are acting like their Father: the God of Peace (Philippians 4:9; 1 Thessalonians 5:23). Peacemakers and those who love their enemies demonstrate their authenticity as children of God by their words and acts of peace. Jesus modeled this by loving us and laying down his life for us, "while we were enemies" (Romans 5:10; cf. Colossians 1:21). After his enemies nailed him to the cross, he prayed, "*Father forgive them*; for they do not know what they are doing" (Luke 23:34).

Therefore, we aspire to demonstrate the gospel with self-giving, sacrificial love toward our Muslim neighbors and toward the small minority of Muslims who might position themselves as our enemies.

9. Differentiate between the Role of Church and State

In Romans 12:9-13:10, Paul described a godly response to evil. He portrayed a sharp contrast between how God's people are to respond to evil versus how the government should respond.

Jesus' followers are called to a peacemaking ethic of sacrificial love. Paul began the section with an appeal to love (Romans 12:9-10) and closed it with a repeated call to loving our neighbor (13:8-10). Moreover, he exhorted believers to bless their persecutors, respond non-violently to evil, and seek peace with all.

By contrast, the state is called to implement justice. Governments stand accountable to God for supporting the good and punishing the evil. The state must address expressions of evil such as terrorism and torture.

Therefore, we distinguish between the role of church and the role of the state.

10. Support and Challenge the State

Followers of Christ should submit to their government, pray for their government (1 Timothy 2:1-4), and support their government's struggle against various manifestations of evil. But exactly how this finds expression varies according to a person's conscience, especially when it comes to "war."

Some of us embrace Pacifism,[44] others Just-War theory,[45] and still others Just-Peacemaking.[46]

Followers of Christ, also, play a prophetic role towards the government. Scripture affirms cases of civil disobedience by God's people (Exodus 1:15-20; Daniel 3:9-18; 6:6-10); the most obvious case illustrated by the apostles who boldly affirmed before the religious authorities, "We must obey God rather than men" (Acts 5:29).

Therefore, we pray for our government and engage politically in accordance with our conscience. We also speak out against governmental policies and practices that we believe are unjust toward Muslims.

Conclusion

These ten affirmations describe how we can be agents of peace in a polarized world. They describe what it means for Peace Catalyst International to truly love Muslims and faithfully bear witness to Christ.

The Grace and Truth Study Guide

Introduction

This study guide is designed to help you wrestle with these issues primarily in a small group or a Sunday school class, but it is also suitable for individual reflection. It is our hope that this study will challenge and inspire you concerning your relationship with Muslims. More importantly, we hope it will help you think biblically about what it means to follow Jesus in the world today. So use this guide as a starting point for discussion. The questions will help you understand the main issues and explore how you or your group might want to either affirm what is written or rewrite portions to make it more in line with your group or organization's thinking.

Some groups will prefer studying the Grace and Truth Exposition (page 15) while others will prefer the Grace and Truth Affirmation (page 25). The questions for each are similar, except that the Exposition contains a section describing the Muslim world.

Study Questions for the Grace and Truth Exposition

For effective discussion, each participant should read the document (or section of the document) beforehand.

➲ Read the entire "Introduction" and "An Accurate and Discerning Look at the Muslim World"
(pages 7-13).

▓ What are some of the issues raised and challenges noted in the
introduction? Which aspects of this are most relevant to you and
why?

▓ Note the chart and brief commentary on the spectrum of
Muslims in the world today (page 8). In what ways, can this chart
help you be more discerning in your understanding of Muslims?
What parts of this chart are most helpful for you? What new
insights (if any) have you gained?

☑ The introduction lists four important points of theological similarity and difference (pages 9-10) between Muslims and Christians. What are some practical implications of the similarities for how we relate to Muslims? What are some practical implications of the differences for how we relate to Muslims?

☑ Concerning the massive diversity described within the Muslim world, what points seem most relevant to you?

☑ How do you feel as you consider the range of diversity among Muslims? How does this impact your understanding? Do you see an understanding of this diversity affecting the issue of fear?

☑ This section closes with a quote from Colin Chapman (page 13). What do you consider to be Chapman's most important point(s)? Are there any points that make you uncomfortable or that you would take issue with on biblical grounds?

Study Questions for the Grace and Truth Exposition

> ➲ Read the first two guidelines: "Be Faithful to God's Truth – the Whole Truth" and "Be Jesus-Centered in our Interaction" (on pages 15-16).

☑ Why are these two guidelines important for Christ-like relationships with Muslims?

☑ Why do you think they are the first two guidelines on the list?

☑ What are the strengths of these guidelines? Weaknesses? Any concerns you have about the content of either of these two guidelines?

☑ Would you like to rewrite any part of these guidelines?

➲ If so, which part? Read the next three guidelines: "Be Truthful and Gracious in our Words and Witness," "Be Wise in our Words and Witness," and "Be Respectful and Bold in our Witness" (on pages 16-19).

☑ Do you think it's important to be both truthful and gracious when speaking about Muslims? Why or why not? How does a Christian commitment to truth and grace impact our interaction with mass media?

☑ How should a Christian commitment to wisdom impact our relationships with Muslims? How should a Christian commitment to wisdom impact our interaction with mass media as it relates to Muslims? What is the role of discernment (biblical critical thinking) as we process information we receive from various sources about Islam or Muslims?

▇ Being both respectful and bold in our witness is easier said than done. The exposition claims that "many of us tend to fall short on one side or the other (or both)." Do you feel that your group (your church, small group, or friends with whom you identify) tends to fall short on one side or the other? If so, where? Do you feel that you personally need to grow in one or both of these areas? What might it look like to become more Christ-like in these ways?

▇ What are the strengths of these three guidelines? Weaknesses? Any concerns you have about the content of any of these three guidelines?

■ Would you like to rewrite any part of these guidelines? If so, which part?

➲ Read the next two guidelines: "Be Prudent in our Google-ized World" and "Be Persistent in our Call for Religious Freedom" (on pages 20-21).

☑ Why is prudence important in a "Google-ized world? Do you agree that Christians should be careful of what they say, because Muslims might "overhear"? What guidelines does Colossians 4:5-6 provide for living in a "Google-ized world? Are there other biblical guidelines you can think of?

☑ Do you have any thoughts about religious freedom for all people? Are there concrete steps you think the Lord might want you or your group to take in this area?

☑ What are the strengths of these guidelines? Weaknesses?
Any concerns you have about the content of either of these two
guidelines?

☑ Would you like to rewrite any part of these guidelines? If so,
which part?

⊃ Read the last two guidelines, "Be Peaceable and Uncompromising in our Dialogue" and "Be Loving toward All" as well as the conclusion (pages 22-24).

☑ What is the value of dialogue? Do you see any dangers in dialogue? If so, how could those be avoided?

☑ How does the guideline about loving neighbors and enemies impact you practically?

How well do you think the church in this country has shown love toward Muslims? How well do you feel you personally have shown love toward Muslims (in attitudes, actions, or words)?

What are the strengths of these guidelines? Weaknesses? Any concerns you have about the content of either of these two guidelines?

✔ Would you like to rewrite any part of these guidelines or the conclusion? If so, which part?

✔ What part of the conclusion is most significant in your mind?

Study Questions for the Grace and Truth Affirmation

⮕ Read the first affirmation: "Be Jesus-Centered in our Interaction" (page 26).

☑ Why is this guideline important for Christ-like relationships with Muslims?

☑ What are the strengths of this guideline? Weaknesses? Any concerns you have about the content of this guideline?

☑ Would you like to rewrite any part of this guideline? If so, which part?

> ➲ Read the next three affirmations: "Be Truthful and Gracious in our Words and Witness," "Be Wise in our Words and Witness," and "Be Respectful and Bold in our Witness" (pages 25-28).

☑ Do you think it's important to be both truthful and gracious when speaking about Muslims? Why or why not? How does a Christian commitment to truth and grace impact our interaction with mass media?

☑ How should a Christian commitment to wisdom impact our relationships with Muslims? How should a Christian commitment to wisdom impact our interaction with mass media, as it relates to Muslims? What is the role of discernment (biblical critical thinking) as we process information we receive from various sources about Islam or Muslims?

☑ Being both respectful and bold in our witness is easier said than done. Do you feel that your group (your church, small group, or friends with whom you identify) tends to fall short in one or the other of these? If so, where? Do you feel that you personally need to grow in one or both of these areas? What might it look like to become more Christ-like in these ways?

☑ What are the strengths of these affirmations? Weaknesses? Any concerns you have about the content of any of these three affirmations?

☑ Would you like to rewrite any part of these affirmations? If so, which part?

⊃ Read the next two affirmations: "Be Prudent in our Glocalized World" and "Be Persistent in our Call for Religious Freedom" (pages 28-29).

▓ Why is prudence important in a "Glocalized" world? Do you agree that Christians should be careful of what they say, because Muslims might "overhear"? What guidelines does Colossians 4:5-6 provide for living in a "Glocalized" world? Are there other biblical guidelines you can think of?

▓ Do you have any thoughts about religious freedom for all people? Are there concrete steps you think the Lord might want you or your group to take in this area?

☑ What are the strengths of these affirmations? Weaknesses? Any concerns you have about the content of either of these two affirmations?

☑ Would you like to rewrite any part of these affirmations? If so, which part?

➲ Read the next two affirmations: "Be Peaceable and Uncompromising in our Dialogue" and "Be Loving toward All" (pages 29-30).

☑ What is the value of dialogue? Do you see any dangers in dialogue? If so, how could those be avoided?

☑ How well do you think the church in this country has shown love toward Muslims? How well do you feel you personally have shown love toward Muslims (in attitudes, actions or words)?

▓ What are the strengths of these affirmations? Weaknesses? Any concerns you have about the content of either of these two affirmations?

▓ Would you like to rewrite any part of these affirmations or the conclusion? If so, which part?

➲ Read the last two affirmations: "Differentiate between the Role of Church and State" and "Support and Challenge the State" (page 31).

☑ Why is it important to "Differentiate between the Role of Church and State?" What are the strengths of this affirmation? The weaknesses? Any concerns you have about its content?

☑ Why is it important to "Support and Challenge the State?" Do you think this additional affirmation would strengthen the document or do you agree it is too controversial to warrant agreement from a wide spectrum of evangelicals?

▓ Would you like to rewrite any part of either of these two affirmations? If so, which part?

Bibliography

The Amman Message Jordan: RABIIT The Royal Aal al-Bayt Institute for Islamic Thought, 2009.

Aslan, Reza. No God but God: The Origins, Evolution, and Future of Islam. New York, NY: Random House, 2006.

Bhutto, Benazir. Reconciliation: Islam, Democracy, and the West. New York, NY: HarperCollins Publisher 2008.

Chapman, Colin. "Christian Responses to Islam, Islamism and 'Islamic Terrorism." Cambridge Papers Vol.16, Number 2, (2007).

Edition, BBC News World, "Falwell 'Sorry' for Mohammed Remark", BBC News World Edition http://news.bbc.co.uk/2/hi/americas/2323897.stm.

Gabriel, Mark A. Islam and Terrorism: What the Quran Really Teaches About Christianity, Violence and the Goals of the Islamic Jihad. Lake Mary, FL: Charisma House, 2002.

Hays, Richard B. The Moral Vision of the New Testament: Community, Cross, New Creation, a Contemporary Introduction to New Testament Ethics. San Francisco, CA: HarperOne, 1996.

Hegeman, Benjamin-Lee. "Beware of Dhimmi Writers." Evangelical Missions Quarterly, no. 301 (2007).

Huckabee, Mike, "On War & Peace: Islamofascism Must Disappear from the Face of the Earth", OnTheIssues. org http://www.ontheissues.org/Archive/2008_CPAC_ Mike_Huckabee.htm (accessed August 29 2013).

Jihad and the Islamic Law of War. Jordan: RABIIT The Royal Aal al-Bayt Institute for Islamic Thought, 2007.

Jordan, The Royal Aal al-Bayt Institute for Islamic Thought in, The Royal Aal al-Bayt Institute for Islamic Thought in Jordan http://www.aalalbayt.org/en/index.html (accessed August 29 2013).

Kamali, Mohammad Hashim. Freedom of Expression in Islam. Cambridge: Islamic Texts Society, 1998.

Kurzman, Charles, "Islamic Statements against Terrorism", unc.edu http://kurzman.unc.edu/islamic-statements-against-terrorism/ (accessed September 3 2013).

Love, Rick. Why Do We Share the Good News About Jesus with All Peoples, Including Muslims? Arvada, CO: ricklove.net, 2004.

_____, "Gracious Christian Responses to Muslims in Britain Today", ricklove.net http://s3.amazonaws.com/ churchplantmedia-cms/peacecatalyst_az/gt-affirmation. pdf (accessed August 28 2013).

McDowell, Bruce and Anees Zaka. Muslims and Christians at the Table: Promoting Biblical Understanding among

North American Muslims. Phillipsburg, NJ: P & R Publishing, 1999.

Medearis, Carl. Muslims, Christians, and Jesus. Grand Rapids, MI: Bethany House 2008.

Movement, The Lausanne, "The Lausanne Covenant", The Lausanne Movement (accessed August 29 2013).

muhajabah.com, "Muslims Condemn Terrorist Attacks", muhajabah.com http://www.muhajabah.com/otherscondemn.php (accessed September 3 2013).

Piper, John. Love Your Enemies (a History of the Tradition and Interpretation of Its Uses): Jesus' Love Command in the Synoptic Gospels and the Early Christian Paraenesis. Wheaton, IL: Crossway, Reprint edition (June 30, 2012).

Plato, "Just War Theory", Stanford.edu http://plato.stanford.edu/entries/war/#2 (accessed August 29 2013).

_____, "Pacifism", Stanford.edu http://plato.stanford.edu/entries/war/#4 (accessed August 29 2013).

princeton.edu, "Islamism", WordNet Search - 3.1 http://wordnetweb.princeton.edu/perl/webwn?s=islamism (accessed August 29 2013).

Roberts, Bob. Glocalization: How Followers of Jesus Engage the New Flat World. Grand Rapids, MI: Zondervan Publishing Company, 2007.

Schwartz, Stephen. The Other Islam: Sufism and the Road to Global Harmony. New York, London, Toronto, Sydney, Auckland: Double Day, 2008.

Singh, David Emmanuel. Jesus and the Cross: Reflections of Christians from Islamic Contexts. Oxford: Regum Books International, 2008.

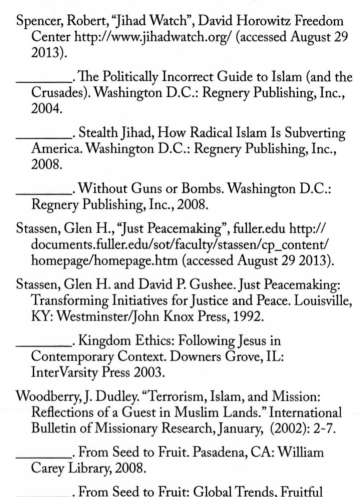

Spencer, Robert, "Jihad Watch", David Horowitz Freedom Center http://www.jihadwatch.org/ (accessed August 29 2013).

_____. The Politically Incorrect Guide to Islam (and the Crusades). Washington D.C.: Regnery Publishing, Inc., 2004.

_____. Stealth Jihad, How Radical Islam Is Subverting America. Washington D.C.: Regnery Publishing, Inc., 2008.

_____. Without Guns or Bombs. Washington D.C.: Regnery Publishing, Inc., 2008.

Stassen, Glen H., "Just Peacemaking", fuller.edu http://documents.fuller.edu/sot/faculty/stassen/cp_content/homepage/homepage.htm (accessed August 29 2013).

Stassen, Glen H. and David P. Gushee. Just Peacemaking: Transforming Initiatives for Justice and Peace. Louisville, KY: Westminster/John Knox Press, 1992.

_____. Kingdom Ethics: Following Jesus in Contemporary Context. Downers Grove, IL: InterVarsity Press 2003.

Woodberry, J. Dudley. "Terrorism, Islam, and Mission: Reflections of a Guest in Muslim Lands." International Bulletin of Missionary Research, January, (2002): 2-7.

_____. From Seed to Fruit. Pasadena, CA: William Carey Library, 2008.

_____. From Seed to Fruit: Global Trends, Fruitful Practices, and Emerging Issues among Muslims. Pasadena, CA: William Carey Library, 2008.

Endnotes

1. Rick Love, "Gracious Christian Responses to Muslims in Britain Today," ricklove.net. http://s3.amazonaws.com/churchplantmedia-cms/peacecatalyst_az/gt-affirmation.pdf (accessed August 28, 2013).

2. For translation into other languages see http://peace-catalyst.net/training/grace--truth.

3. We take seriously God's admonition to "be at peace with all people" (Rom 12:18; Heb 12:14).

4. We are focusing on Muslims instead of an academic study of the religion of Islam. Certainly a focus on people who adhere to the religion of Islam means that we will be concerned about their beliefs. But we are focusing on actual Muslim people because ministry is primarily about relationship. What counts is how Muslims actually live and apply their religious system to their daily lives.

5. J. Dudley Woodberry, "Terrorism, Islam, and Mission: Reflections of a Guest in Muslim Lands," *International Bulletin of Missionary Research, January*, (2002): 2-7. The Qur'an comprises recitations by Muhammad, believed to come from God, to meet the needs that arose on specific occasions. Some were peaceful; others were not. Therefore, either position can be argued by

selecting specific verses from the Qur'an or illustrations from history.

6.   J. Dudley Woodberry, *From Seed to Fruit: Global Trends, Fruitful Practices, and Emerging Issues among Muslims* (Pasadena, CA: William Carey Library, 2008), 6. We do well to avoid stereotyping Muslims based on news sound bites or the reductionism of focusing primarily on religion as the cause of conflicts between Muslim and Christian communities. There are many perspectives in the Muslim community, and even these are changing. Conflicts between Muslim and Christian communities in places like Indonesia and Sudan have ethnic, economic, and political, as well as religious, roots.

7.   *Jihad and the Islamic Law of War*, (Jordan: RABIIT The Royal Aal al-Bayt Institute for Islamic Thought, 2007), 58-60. These five categories are taken, with names simplified for this book. It is impossible to get a precise percentage of the various categories, but this chart helps capture visually something of the number of Muslims in each category.

8.   Mohammad Hashim Kamali, *Freedom of Expression in Islam* (Cambridge: Islamic Texts Society, 1998). This book is an excellent example of a traditionalist addressing a massively important topic (which includes freedom of religion and the law of apostasy).

9.   Shariah law refers to a legal system based on Islamic principles of jurisprudence. Shariah law addresses many aspects of day-to-day life, including politics, economics, banking, business, contracts, family, sexuality, hygiene, and social issues.

10.   Muslims, of course, add the Qur'ān to this list, whereas Christians believe that the canon of Scripture closed with the Bible. Also, Muslims do not necessarily interpret the meaning of some of the terms in these points as Christians do – see the

points of disagreement immediately below."

11. The Qur'ān contains verses, which encourage loving friendship with Christians (e.g., al-Mā'ida [5]:82), and others, which seem to discourage friendship with Christians (e.g,. al-Mā'ida [5]:51), as well as others, which note that not all Christians are alike (e.g., Āl 'Imrān [3]:113-115).

12. Also, verses such as 1 Pet 3:8,9; Matt 22:39 and numerous others. The positive effect these virtues can have on Muslim-Christian relations is acknowledged in Qur'anic verses such as al-Mā'ida [5]:82 – "You will find the nearest people in love toward those who have believed [i.e., Muslims] are those who say, 'We are Christians.' That is because among them are clergy and monks, and they are not arrogant."

13. *The Amman Message* (Jordan: RABIIT The Royal Aal al-Bayt Institute for Islamic Thought, 2009), 16-17. This book refers to four Sunnī schools (*madhāhib*) and four non-Sunnī schools.

14. princeton.edu, "Islamism," WordNet Search - 3.1. http://wordnetweb.princeton.edu/perl/webwn?s=islamism (accessed August 29, 2013). Islamism - "a fundamentalist Islamic revivalist movement generally characterized by moral conservatism and the literal interpretation of the Koran and the attempt to implement Islamic values in all aspects of life."

15. For example: The Royal Aal al-Bayt Institute for Islamic Thought in Jordan, The Royal Aal al-Bayt Institute for Islamic Thought in Jordan http://www.aalalbayt.org/en/index.html (accessed August 29, 2013). In addition see: Kamali. See also the following: Reza Aslan, *No God but God: The Origins, Evolution, and Future of Islam* (New York, NY: Random House, 2006). And Benazir Bhutto, *Reconciliation: Islam, Democracy, and the West* (New York, NY: HarperCollins Publisher 2008).

16. Stephen Schwartz, *The Other Islam: Sufism and the Road to Global Harmony* (New York, London, Toronto, Sydney, Auckland: Double Day, 2008).

17. See, Charles Kurzman, "Islamic Statements against Terrorism," unc.edu. http://kurzman.unc.edu/islamic-statements-against-terrorism/ (accessed September 3, 2013). See also, muhajabah.com, "Muslims Condemn Terrorist Attacks," muhajabah.com. http://www.muhajabah.com/otherscondemn.php (accessed September 3, 2013).

18. Adjusted with the author's permission, from its original reading: "(e) demonstrating a fundamental respect for Islam (without agreeing with all its teaching)."

19. Colin Chapman, "Christian Responses to Islam, Islamism and 'Islamic Terrorism," *Cambridge Papers* Vol.16, Number 2, (2007): 5.

20. The Lausanne Movement, "The Lausanne Covenant," The Lausanne Movement. (accessed August 29, 2013). This commitment corresponds to the Lausanne Covenant's declaration: "World evangelization requires the whole Church to take the whole gospel to the whole world."

21. Carl Medearis, *Muslims, Christians, and Jesus* (Grand Rapids, MI: Bethany House 2008). See Medearis for an example of this approach.

22. Bob Roberts, *Glocalization: How Followers of Jesus Engage the New Flat World* (Grand Rapids, MI: Zondervan Publishing Company, 2007), 255.

23. Love.

24. Mike Huckabee, "On War & Peace: Islamofascism Must Disappear from the Face of the Earth," OnTheIssues.org. http://

www.ontheissues.org/Archive/2008_CPAC_Mike_Huckabee. htm (accessed August 29, 2013). From a USA presidential candidate and evangelical pastor: "It is right for us to be on the offense against Islamofascism, and not wait until they attack us on our soil. Unlike any war we have ever fought in this nation, this is not a war for soil. It is a war for our soul. We will either win it or we will lose it. This nation must rally to the point where we recognize there is no compromise. There is no alternative. We must win; they must lose. Islamofascism must disappear from the face of the earth, or we will."

25. Of course, the golden rule mandates that we acknowledge the historical and current weaknesses and problems within Christendom as well as those within Islam.

26. Benjamin-Lee Hegeman, "Beware of *Dhimmi* Writers," Evangelical Missions Quarterly, no. 301 (2007): 432-439. Hegeman expounds well on the "fear factor" in this article," in which he writes: "Fear left untreated turns to hatred and both defensive writers and *dhimmi* writers leave the reader's fear intact. Engagement writers take one beyond one's fears."

27. Robert Spencer, "Jihad Watch," David Horowitz Freedom Center. http://www.jihadwatch.org/ (accessed August 29, 2013). Spenser is the author of Jihad Watch as well as books such as: Robert Spencer, *The Politically Incorrect Guide to Islam (and the Crusades)* (Washington D.C.: Regnery Publishing, Inc., 2004). Robert Spencer, *Stealth Jihad, How Radical Islam Is Subverting America* (Washington D.C.: Regnery Publishing, Inc., 2008). And Robert Spencer, *Without Guns or Bombs* (Washington D.C.: Regnery Publishing, Inc., 2008).

28. The Lord's command to "contend for the faith" (Jude 3) does not imply doing so in a contentious way, but rather as described in 2 Tim 2:24-26: "And the Lord's servant… must be *kind* to

everyone....Those who oppose him he must *gently* instruct…"
(NIV, emphasis added).

29. J. Dudley Woodberry, *From Seed to Fruit* (Pasadena, CA: William Carey Library, 2008). See Joseph Cumming's helpful article, "Toward Respectful Witness," 311-324

30. Mark A. Gabriel, *Islam and Terrorism: What the Quran Really Teaches About Christianity, Violence and the Goals of the Islamic Jihad* (Lake Mary, FL: Charisma House, 2002), 200. Gabriel (former professor of Islamic history at Al-Azhar University) tends to be critical of Islam. Yet, when it comes to sharing the gospel he admonishes us: "Never denigrate Muhammad or the Quran … Respect their customs and sensitivities."

31. David Emmanuel Singh, Jesus and the Cross: Reflections of Christians from Islamic Contexts (Oxford: Regum Books International, 2008: 125-133). See Haw Yung's "The Parable of the Waiting Father" (Luke15:11-32) through the cultural value of honor (and shame) rather than the guilt perspective of the prodigal son's sin. Methodist bishop Hwa Yung illustrates a respectful and bold witness of the cross that reflects the culture of the original gospel story and approaches Muslims in their cultural perspective.

32. Rick Love, "Why Do We Share the Good News About Jesus with All Peoples, Including Muslims?" (http://www.ricklove.net/wp-content/uploads/2010/04/Why-we-share-the-good-news-with-Muslims.pdf) (accessed September 19, 2013)

33. BBC News World Edition, "Falwell 'Sorry' for Mohammed Remark," BBC News World Edition. http://news.bbc.co.uk/2/hi/americas/2323897.stm.

34. John Piper, *Love Your Enemies (a History of the Tradition and Interpretation of Its Uses): Jesus' Love Command in the Synoptic*

Gospels and the Early Christian Paraenesis (Wheaton, IL: Crossway, Reprint edition (June 30, 2012)).

35. One of the terms used to describe how Paul the apostle communicated is *dialegomai* (usually translated as reason, argue or discuss; Acts 17:2,17; 18:4,19; 19:8,9; 20:7,9; 24:12,25). According to the standard Greek Lexicon (BDAG), *dialegomai* means: "to engage in speech interchange, converse, discuss, argue esp. of instructional discourse that frequently includes exchange of opinions." Dialogue was one of the means Paul used to share the gospel.

36. Bruce and Anees Zaka McDowell, *Muslims and Christians at the Table: Promoting Biblical Understanding among North American Muslims* (Phillipsburg, NJ: P & R Publishing, 1999). These authors provide one good example that encourages Christ-honoring Muslim-Christian dialogue at the local level.

37. For various ways to interpret to interpret, see: Glen H. and David P. Gushee Stassen, *Kingdom Ethics: Following Jesus in Contemporary Context* (Downers Grove, IL: InterVarsity Press 2003), 128f. See also: Richard B. Hays, *The Moral Vision of the New Testament: Community, Cross, New Creation, a Contemporary Introduction to New Testament Ethics* (San Francisco, CA: HarperOne, 1996), 320-324

38. Hays, 343. Hays argues that the problem is not hermeneutics but lack of obedience: "One reason the world finds the New Testament's message of peacemaking and love of enemies incredible is that the church is so massively faithless."

39. Glen H. and David P. Gushee Stassen, *Just Peacemaking: Transforming Initiatives for Justice and Peace* (Louisville, KY: Westminster/John Knox Press, 1992), 33-88. See also: Stassen, *Kingdom Ethics: Following Jesus in Contemporary Context*, 125-145.

40. Hays, 326.

41. Ibid., 332. "From Matthew to Revelation, we find a consistent witness against violence and a calling to the community to follow the example of Jesus in *accepting* suffering rather than *inflicting* it."

42. Globalization radically defines and shapes life in the twenty-first[t] century. One important new way of describing globalization is the term "glocalization." "Glocalization" combines the words "global" and "local" to highlight the comprehensive connectedness of the world in which we live. What happens among the nations impacts our neighbors, and what happens among our neighbors impacts the nations.

43. See http://www.desiringgod.org/resource-library/sermons/subjection-to-god-and-subjection-to-the-state-part-4 (accessed September 19, 2013).

44. Plato, "Pacifism," Stanford.edu. http://plato.stanford.edu/entries/war/#4 (accessed August 29, 2013).

45. Plato, "Just War Theory," Stanford.edu. http://plato.stanford.edu/entries/war/#2 (accessed August 29, 2013).

46. Glen H. Stassen, "Just Peacemaking Paradigm," fuller.edu. http://justpeacemaking.org/the-practices/ (accessed August 29, 2013).

CPSIA information can be obtained at www.ICGtesting.com
Printed in the USA
LVOW12s2342131013

356715LV00001B/1/P